Good Morning, God

Photographed and hand painted by Kathleen Francour
Stories by Sylvia Seymour

Photography: © 1997 Kathleen Francour
Carefree, Arizona. All rights reserved.

ISBN: 0-7853-2116-0

PUBLICATIONS INTERNATIONAL, LTD.
7373 North Cicero Avenue
Lincolnwood, Illinois 60646

Rise and Shine

Lucy did not want to get up. It was too early. Why couldn't she sleep a little longer? She dragged herself out of bed and stood looking out of her window. The sun was like a tiny face peeking over the tree tops.

"Hello, Sun," Lucy said yawning. "Do you hate to wake up, too?"

The sun was bigger now, spreading its light across the sky like a gentle smile.

"Lucy," Mother called, "breakfast is ready."

She stretched sleepily and thought about the tasty breakfast waiting for her downstairs. She smiled at the happy sun and whispered, "Thank you, Jesus, for the morning sun. And thank you for this new day."

I am small,
my heart is clean;
let no one dwell in it
except God alone.

This morning, God,
this is Your day.
I am Your child.
Show me Your way.

   Amen.

Lord Jesus Christ, be with me today,
    And help me in all I think, and do, and say.

O God, Creator of Light,
At the rising of Your sun this morning,
let the greatest of all light, Your love,
rise like the sun within our hearts.

                    Amen.

A Surprise for Mommy

"I'll surprise Mommy this morning!" Johnny whispered happily. "I'm a big boy and I can get dressed by myself." He wiggled his head and arms through his pullover shirt and stepped into his shorts. They were a little bit crooked, but the tag was in the back like Mom said.

Johnny pulled on his socks. "Now, which shoe?" he thought. "Jesus will help me. He always helps me when I ask Him." Johnny closed his eyes and prayed. "Dear Jesus, please help me find the right shoe." He put his foot into his shoe. It fit! The other shoe was a perfect fit, too.

"Look Mommy," called Johnny. "I did it! I did it!"

Good morning, Lord!
Be with me all day long,
until the shadows lengthen,
and the evening comes,
and the hustle and bustle of life is done,
and those at work are back at home.
Then in Thy mercy, grant us safe lodging,
and a Holy rest, and peace at the last.

Amen.

Lord, teach us to pray.

I have a busy day today, Jesus.
Help me to do my chores with cheer
and be kind to others,
even if they are not kind to me.
Watch over me as I walk the dog
and play with my friends.
Lord, I have a busy day.
Thank you for being by my side.

Amen.

The First Day of School

When Robert saw the big school building and all the children, he whispered to his mother, "Do I have to go?"

"Yes, Robert," Mother said softly as she put her arms around him. "I know that you are nervous about your first day at school. Let's pray to Jesus to look out for you today." Mother and Robert prayed that he would not be lonely or scared at school. They walked through the school's big front door. When they reached his classroom, he heard a friendly voice.

"Hi, Robert," Scott called.

Robert's face broke into a smile when he saw his friend. "Are you in this class, too?" He wasn't afraid anymore. God sent him a friend.

The year's at the spring
   And day's at the morn;
Morning's at seven;
   The hillside's dew-pearl'd;
The lark's on the wing;
   The snail's on the thorn;
God's in His heaven—
   All is right with the world.

Robert Browning

The Lord is all I need.
He takes care of me.

Psalm 16:5

For this new morning and its light,
    For rest and shelter of the night,
For health and food, for love and friends,
    For every gift Your goodness sends,
We thank You, gracious Lord.

This is the day which the Lord has made;
let us rejoice and be glad in it.

Psalm 118:24

Dear Father,

As we start this day, please guide us.

Please help Mom and Dad as they work.

Please help me at school.

Please help my little sister at home,

and all my other friends and family.

Amen.